Dear Life

Praying through the year
with Christian Aid

Janet Morley
Hannah Ward
Jennifer Wild

First published in Great Britain 1998

Christian Aid
PO Box 100
London SE1 7RT

Cover photo: Kusumabi Charan, sister of Moti (p19).
Christian Aid/Harriet Logan/Network

Designed by SHOP, London
Printed by Blackmore Ltd, Shaftesbury, Dorset

British Library Cataloguing-in-Publication Data
A catalogue record for this book is available from the British Library.
ISBN 0-904379-31-0

Contents

April **Building communities**

May **Supporters in the United Kingdom and Ireland**

June **Food security**

July **Water**

August **Small enterprise loans**

September **Emergencies**

October **Basic rights**

November **Land and environment**

December **Health**

Introduction

'In different parts of the world there are people who serve God and who pray for the whole world. We might not know them directly but we want them to pray for us.'

These are the words of an Ethiopian priest but they express a longing for connection through prayer which many of us share, wherever we live in the world. Those individuals who seek to pray for each other using this book will be doing so from a variety of contexts – not only different parts of the United Kingdom and Ireland, where Christian Aid is based, but from the other communities whose lives and work are introduced here. Partner organisations who are featured here will all receive copies of this book, which invites prayer for Christian Aid supporters in the UK and Ireland as well as for projects overseas. All of us who are represented in the book will be strengthened by knowing there is a wide community of prayer focusing on our situation at around the same time of year.

Dear Life seeks to offer a way of encountering others whom we do not know face to face but want to pray for. The idea is to spend time with the visual images in this book, to let them function as 'icons' – images which we seek to enter in imagination and in the presence of God, images which are not just looked at but in some way look back at us, the viewer. In specific situations and on the faces of particular people we recognise our common humanity – weaknesses exposed and strengths called forth. We open ourselves to a sense of mutual exchange of sympathy and understanding. The words on the page are supplied to support this kind of prayer: information about the person and their community; a biblical quote, with a wider reference to look up, to help 'earth' our reflections within Christian tradition; and a worded prayer which draws on all the elements of a page to focus a meditative response in the reader/viewer.

The world in which we offer prayer is full of injustices and inequalities. Many people are trapped in poverty and unable to realise ordinary human aspirations: having an adequate and secure home, finding a means of earning a living, being able to put food on the table, raising healthy children and educating them. The continuing poverty of communities and nations is often not due to accidents of climate, but to global economic systems controlled by wealthier nations and institutions. Trading systems that benefit the rich, and the unrepayable foreign debts which paralyse the economies of poorer nations, play a large part in perpetuating poverty. Money is diverted to interest repayments that could otherwise have been spent on health and education.

As a response to poverty in our world, some people feel that prayer as such is beside the point, compared with the need for immediate concrete action, such as giving money or campaigning for political change. But Christian Aid understands prayer to be an essential part of the threefold response that is demanded of us: to *give* of our resources to help people raise themselves from poverty in specific local situations; to *act* by putting pressure on decision-makers to change the underlying causes that keep people poor; but also to *pray* – to seek to enter, in heart, mind and imagination, the situations of our brothers and sisters whom we have not met; to place ourselves alongside their suffering and their strength, and to ask for God's promises for a different world to be fulfilled in us and in them.

So far from being a passive or soft option, prayer underpins the other responses we make to the world. If we pray honestly and with open hearts, we shall not be able to escape the questions about how we personally apportion our money, or whether we are actually using our influence to bring about change. But prayer also protects us – from the illusion that we can change things entirely under our own power, and from the burnout that comes from believing that we must. When we pray we are asking to place ourselves and those for whom we pray together under the power of God; and we know that we are not alone. Correspondingly, anyone who has had the experience of being prayed for in times of difficulty and distress can testify to the huge strength and comfort it brings. It is powerful to know that others outside our own situation, who could choose to stay at a distance, want to come close in heart and imagination, and understand what we are facing. We ask this of each other; we offer this to each other; those praying and those prayed for are mutually helped.

Praying for the world is a strong activity; it is work for grown-ups, for those of us who are not afraid to risk knowing about our own helplessness and mortality, as well as our strengths, or to contemplate steadily the evils in which we are all involved. It is for those who have decided to choose hope, in a world where despair often has, on the surface, the more convincing arguments. It is for those who want to celebrate our connectedness with sisters and brothers across the world, so that, in a world where life is often held cheap, we may all come to cherish 'dear life'.

Issues for prayer month by month

We have divided the work of Christian Aid and its partners under different headings according to each month. This is for the sake of clarity and simplicity of focus for the reader. Over the course of the year, the whole range of development priorities Christian Aid seeks to support will have been considered. However, it is important to realise that very few of the programmes funded have only one priority. There are usually multiple reasons why communities are poor and find it hard to move out of poverty, and a good programme will address several causes of poverty simultaneously. For instance, good nutrition and health for small children is achieved not only by providing places where they can receive supplementary meals, but by ensuring health education for their mothers, and a means for women to earn an income so as to implement what they learn. Issues are strongly interrelated. Access to clean water is vital for everyone's health, but it can also significantly free up time for girls and women, to enable them to get an education. And so on; you will find that in many cases, programmes that are under one heading might just as easily be placed under another. But the headings represent important themes that emerge again and again when we consider poverty and how it can be tackled.

January: Children

Nothing is more important than what poverty is doing to the world's children. Beyond the immediate struggle for life – infant deaths are very high – and their present hunger, children's growth and future health and energy are at stake during their early years. Learning is vital; are children getting access to the skills they need to make the most of their lives and become responsible and contented citizens? Or are they learning fear and humiliation, becoming brutalised by conflict or enforced prostitution? Is there space and time to play, or do their families depend on their labour before their bodies are fully formed? Christian Aid supports programmes that tackle all these issues: combating infant malnutrition in intensive feeding clinics; giving additional support in literacy to children and adults for whom primary education has been disrupted; offering a 'safe house' for street children to find ways out of prostitution; and space to play for children who must work to assist their families, or who, on release from bonded labour, need help with re-entry into normal life.

February: Conflict

Internal conflict, which may rage for many years, often happens in countries where a large proportion of the population lives in poverty, and where there is a marked gap between rich and poor. In the first instance, conflict often creates an immediate need for emergency relief. But even beyond the crisis, conflict leaves people displaced, uprooting them from their secure communities and support systems, requiring them to find new skills and markets in order to survive. It frequently leaves a legacy of continuing unintended violence in its wake – landmines, sown throughout the world's conflict zones like dragon's teeth, wait to maim and kill civilians for years to come, crippling whole populations. Conflict often destroys the infrastructures which maintain life: wells and roads are sometimes targeted for destruction as each side seeks to manipulate people's support. After conflict has been resolved, poor countries often find they are unable to undertake proper reconstruction of their economies. Deeply in debt to foreign governments, they are required to cut this sort of spending, in order to meet their ever-increasing interest repayments. Christian Aid supports programmes which address the legacy of conflict, in terms of both practical problems and the issues around reconciliation.

March: Women

Throughout the world women are among the poorest of the poor. They universally earn lower average wages than men for the work they do, and spend more hours on domestic labour, while receiving less respect. Girls are given less to eat, receive less education and are given much less choice about what they may do with their lives. As a result of powerlessness and lack of economic independence, women may find it hard to defend themselves if they are subject to domestic violence. Yet they are also typically the farmers who produce the food the family eats; and they are usually the ones who continue to care for their children under the most difficult circumstances, even when their menfolk have given up the struggle and departed. Most women are multi-skilled and have considerable powers of endurance, flexibility and commitment. Finding ways to give women confidence, self-respect and the capacity to earn an income is crucial in improving the life of whole communities.

April: Building communities

It is often the case that the churches take a lead, not only in encouraging practical development work, but in finding ways to address those less tangible problems which nevertheless have a profound impact on the life of their society. In situations where conflict has been a part of life for decades, or where there are cultural or ethnic divides that have their roots in colonial history, people often have to tackle much more than physical poverty. Communities who have been regarded as inferior, with fewer rights and less respect than other groups, need to have their confidence built up through learning about, and learning to take pride in, their own heritage. Sometimes there are painful memories of violence or oppression to be worked with, if previously opposed groups are to find a way of building normal community life together. Where a community is Christian, biblical reflection is often a powerful tool for drawing people together and finding inspiration for the future in the face of difficult circumstances in daily life. People who are to lift themselves out of poverty and create a society where old conflicts will not re-ignite need to have a strong sense of their own dignity.

May: Supporters in the United Kingdom and Ireland

Since Christian Aid Week falls each year in May, we are asking for prayer for all those who support the work of Christian Aid then and throughout the year in a variety of ways. Many (though not all) supporters are active members of their local church and have been drawn into involvement through that route. Forty church denominations officially sponsor Christian Aid and help to guide its policy. Altogether there are about 275 employed staff and more than 300,000 volunteers across England, Wales, Scotland and Ireland (Northern Ireland and the Republic). As they learn about what makes and keeps people poor in the world, people are invited to respond in three key ways: giving, acting and praying. Fundraising is absolutely vital in order to enable Christian Aid to do its work of funding the projects featured in this book and many more. But, with so many of the constraints which prevent communities escaping from poverty stemming from global economic forces, campaigning about these must also be a priority. And prayer underpins our work and protects us from despair.

June: Food security

The basic daily human task is feeding ourselves and our families. How easy or difficult this is depends on a variety of factors. Some people struggle with a difficult natural environment, which may be prone to drought or flood, or have poor and infertile soil. Traditional farming methods using indigenous crop varieties have often managed to work with climate or soil problems. But modern agribusiness practice, focusing on huge areas of a single crop, using artificial insecticides and cutting down swathes of forest, has often altered the climate and denuded the soil entirely. Where countries have a high foreign debt, there are incentives to grow single crops for export rather than a variety for home consumption. Often after conflict the rural infrastructure of roads and bridges is damaged and local markets destroyed, so that people cannot trade the crops they grow for the other items they need for a balanced diet.

Many of the projects Christian Aid funds seek to support farming methods that restore to people a secure source of food which they are reliably able to supply for themselves. This can be through creating kitchen gardens with immediate variety or through developing a crop that is marketable locally. Using natural methods to fertilise the soil and repel pests protects the environment for future generations and means that people do not have to become dependent on expensive foreign inputs.

July: Water

Water is the basis of all life for animals, plants and people. This may be why the need for convenient access to water is one of the most well-understood development issues. Collecting water is commonly the task of women, and it is hard to over-estimate the amount of women's time that is wasted each day on this job, not to mention the punishment their bodies take in the process. Health and water are strongly linked. Adequate sanitation and a clean source of drinking water, free from pollution by animals, are both essential to combat disease. In a hot climate where there is no nearby water source, people will often not drink enough, and suffer urinary tract infections as a result. Sometimes a traditional source of water becomes polluted by industrial mining or production processes. In all of these circumstances Christian Aid funds programmes which help people with advocacy or with technical assistance so that communities can provide their own clean source of water.

August: Small enterprise loans

One of the major difficulties people have in lifting themselves out of poverty is that banks do not regard them as a good credit risk. This means that people cannot get started on even a very small-scale enterprise which would enable them to generate an income for their families. Alternatively, they have to accept the astronomical interest rates offered by loan sharks, and risk getting themselves into irremediable debt as a result, if the business does not immediately take off. Christian Aid funds programmes which can provide start-up loans to be paid back on a realistic schedule as the harvest comes in or the business succeeds. Often the scheme works on a savings and loans basis; people contribute when they are able, and then take out loans when they need them. Thus people become self-sufficient by their own efforts, and by 'recycling' money. Sometimes the loans will be in kind rather than cash. In many rural communities, expensive working animals like donkeys and water buffaloes are loaned for ploughing and transporting crops. As the animals breed, their offspring are loaned on to other communities or individuals.

September: Emergencies

Christian Aid puts a strong emphasis on funding long-term development plans, but there will always be emergency situations that flare up. In these situations, funds are instantly made available wherever there are partners who can address the local impact of the emergency. These may be partners of Christian Aid, or may work via ACT International (Action by Churches Together), the worldwide ecumenical network for response to emergencies, to which Christian Aid belongs. In all cases consideration is given, not only to supplying immediate needs, but to the next set of problems that will arise if unplanned for. For instance, seeds and tools for sowing next year's harvest if the crop has failed are just as important as emergency feeding centres in a crisis. Some parts of the world suffer regular and reasonably predictable severe weather patterns: flood, cyclone and drought. Here programmes have invested in emergency preparations, which can save lives and mitigate the worst effects if disaster strikes. However, changing weather patterns due to global warming (eg a more severe 'El Niño' effect) are making prediction harder.

October: Basic rights

People who are poor are not in a good position to insist on some of the basic human rights which others take for granted. If you are desperate to feed your children you will accept any wage or any price for your crop that you are offered. If it is a choice between that and seeing them starve you may even agree to let your children become bonded labourers. Peasants whose families have farmed the same fields for generations may find their traditional but unwritten rights to the land challenged by rich entrepreneurs, foreign businesses or even unsympathetic governments. Christian Aid funds programmes that engage in legal advocacy for poor communities whose rights, freedom and access to utilities are curtailed. These programmes may also give encouragement to popular campaigns aimed at turning laws on the statute book that benefit the poor into reality on the ground. Where there is a trading link with the UK and Ireland, Christian Aid encourages people there to campaign by using their purchasing power, for instance by buying only fairly traded coffee which gives a fair price to the small farmers who produce the crop, or by lobbying supermarkets to produce a code of practice relating to all the goods they purchase.

November: Land and environment

For many of the world's communities, access to land or coastal waters is crucial to long-term survival. Sometimes it is hard for city-dwellers to appreciate how strongly people's identity can be bound up with the land which they cultivate, and which nourishes them. However, traditional ways of life which involved working the land or fishing the water in a sustainable way are often under threat. So food sources which replenished themselves in the forest or the seas are over-exploited by large vested interests using high-tech methods. This results in a polluted environment in which the balance of nature is destroyed, species disappear, and poor people who might once have survived now go hungry. Christian Aid funds programmes that work for the benefit of such people, seeking ways to restore environments and prevent future exploitation.

December: Health

People who are not well cannot work. For those whose only source of wealth is the labour of their bodies, this is the difference between life and death. And yet many of the diseases suffered by the poor could be prevented or treated relatively cheaply. In most places the only cushion in times of sickness is the extended family, who 'share the poverty' and support relatives who are ill. These days this can be a devastating drain on resources. Countries who are deeply in debt to foreign governments have been required to divert money previously devoted to primary health care into paying interest repayments. So the rising cost of medical care and drugs, even if available, is a nightmare for a poor family. People will usually wait until illness is far advanced before seeking treatment, and this may mean a poorer prognosis or more expensive treatment. Many poor countries cannot undertake serious programmes to combat the spread of AIDS and to treat it; the impact of the disease on future generations is incalculable, as the breadwinners of families die in young adulthood. Christian Aid funds a range of health programmes: support of home-based care for the dying, health education in nutrition and hygiene to prevent many common conditions; village health workers who move around and offer primary health care; and encouragement of herbal remedies which are easily available and draw on traditional local wisdom about health cures.

Choosing which programmes to fund

Christian Aid helps poor communities by funding locally run programmes which have been carefully assessed. It usually only works through expatriate staff in the few situations where there is no viable local organisation through whom to work, or where, because of civil unrest, a field officer who is not identified with local politics can help with communication. In these cases, building up local capacity is a first priority.

In this book you will find featured 44 of the overseas programmes we fund. Overall Christian Aid gives grants to over 600 programmes in 60 countries. Almost all the programmes are organised by local groups (often but not always church based) who are best able to analyse and address the needs of the communities in which they work. Priorities for funding include:

- concrete benefits for the poorest and most excluded members of the community
- a well thought-out, cost-effective programme, with clear objectives so that achievements can be measured
- methods that enable people to develop skills and help themselves long term, rather than become dependent
- improvement in the position of women
- methods of working that are sustainable, that enhance the environment and do not harm it
- the capacity to analyse the causes of poverty, and work with similar programmes to create an effective local pressure group about issues that affect the poor.

January

Children

Christian Aid/Mike Goldwater/Network

Karen refugee children on the Thai/Burmese border

Raipur, central India

Children who work

Life is serious for 12-year-old Moti Charan. Here he has found a customer who needs his shoe-shining skills, but sometimes he has to walk up to eight miles round his home town of Raipur in central India, looking for custom, and he does this six days a week. As with other child labourers, Moti's family depends on his earnings, supplementing those of his father, a roadside cobbler, to buy food for the family. Even with Moti's labours the family has too little to eat, and Moti himself is often too tired in the evenings to go to the classes organised by Christian Aid's partner, the Raipur Churches Development and Relief Committee (RCDRC). A basic education offers the only hope of a better life for dalits – India's poorest people – such as Moti's family.

Moti is rightly proud of his contribution to the family's income and health – but on Sundays he and other child labourers have a chance to enjoy something of the freedom of childhood for a day, when RCDRC takes them to a park and provides not only a meal but a chance for them to play their favourite games and learn some new ones.

Below the level of my sight,
I find the lowly tasks are done
not just by those who are poor,
but by the children –
responsible, serious,
shouldering the adult burden
before they are fully grown.
God give them time to play,
and live, and dream,
as I am free to do.

Christian Aid/Harriet Logan/Network

'This was the manifesto of Jesus Christ. It holds out hope to the hopeless.'

Rajendra Sail, RCDRC, commenting on the Bible passage Luke 4:18-19

Luke 4:18-19 (Isaiah 61:1-2) The Spirit of the Lord is upon me, because he has anointed me to bring good news to the poor. (v18)

‘When I began working with the girls, they used to tell me the streets were the passage to hell – because only people like them live there – street children, prostitutes, people who take drugs. So that’s why I asked them to help me build a space that would be a passage to heaven.’

Ana Vasconcelos, founder and Director of Passage House

Christian Aid/Judith Crouch

Recife, Brazil

Street girls

Tender God,
lover of humankind,
you wore our flesh,
and know its pain, its pride.
Remember these children,
forced by poverty to sell it.
Restore their dignity, and mine.
Give us our bodies back.

'We have written a play about how life is for girls living and working on the street. I love this work – I'm representing all street girls, not just myself – and they need a voice.' (Olivia)

Millions of children and young people are forced to live and work on the streets of Brazil's major cities. About 30 per cent of these street children are girls, most of whom come from very poor families. Some have been abandoned by parents unable to look after them; some have left home because they have been sexually abused by male members of their families. Once on the streets, life is even harder, and girls are particularly at risk. Forced into drug dealing and petty crime, they frequently end up turning to prostitution just to survive.

Ana Vasconcelos encountered some of these girls in her work as a lawyer and set up Casa de Passagem – Passage House – in response to their plight. Based in the port of Recife, Passage House gives girls a way out from life on the streets and a chance to regain their self-esteem. It offers food, counselling, medical help, skills training, and education on issues such as AIDS, drugs, housing, unemployment and women's rights – and, of course, a chance to inform others about life on the streets through the street theatre group shown in the picture.

Matthew 18:10-14

It is not the will of your Father in heaven that one of these little ones should be lost. (v14)

The Gaza Strip,
Palestinian Territories

Informal education

'My teacher told me about the centre and arranged for me to come. I love playing football here and I've made lots of friends. I've always enjoyed reading – especially cultural stories about Palestine. There is lots of freedom here but I really want to learn. Arabic is my favourite lesson, and I want to be a medical doctor.'

Esam El Zagzog, 13-year-old user of the teenagers' centre

Progress in reading is difficult when you have missed a lot of schooling, like these Palestinian children who live in the Gaza Strip, one of the most fought-over places in history. Repeated curfews and school closures have seriously disrupted their education.

Today Gaza contains many refugee camps and is one of the poorest and most densely populated places in the world. The Palestinian Authority does not have sufficient funds to support education and health services. Some children suffer malnutrition, and many no longer attend school because their parents cannot afford books and uniforms. Schools have virtually no equipment and can cope only by taking children in half-day sessions.

These two boys attend a teenagers' centre (Boonat Al Ghad – Builders of Tomorrow Club) run by a local organisation, the Culture and Free Thought Association. As well as getting help with their reading there is also space at the centre to socialise and play sport. Young people who come here learn to be responsible for themselves and for others. They learn to make decisions and take trips to possible work places. The teenagers themselves tell the centre what they need and it tries to provide it.

Christian Aid/DK Crevance

O God, deliver our world
from the recurring conflicts
that close borders,
close schools,
close minds,
and shut off the future.
Give the children freedom
to learn from their heritage,
read their own language,
and take pride in their people.

Mark 12:28-34 You shall love the Lord your God with all your heart, and with all your soul, and with all your mind, and with all your strength... You shall love your neighbour as yourself. (v30-31)

Gillian Weeks

'Without Gemini this would have been so much worse. Now at least I have someone to support me and share my problems.'

Mother of twins, Addis Ababa

Addis Ababa, Ethiopia

Supporting families with twins

Motherly God,
in whose arms are held
all who cry out to you:
teach me to open my heart, my home,
even when I have little to give,
to make room for all your children
and give them space to grow.

Two mothers, two sets of twins – you can just see the fourth child peeping out from behind his mother on the left. Do you wonder at first if they have been gathered into this tiny space for the benefit of the camera? Actually, they live in this old kiosk, a space barely big enough for the sleeping mat they all share.

In Addis Ababa, the arrival of twins is often the last straw for poor families, and Fikre's husband, a casual labourer, has departed, unable to cope with *two* extra mouths to feed. Fikre's babies might have starved, but she found help from the Gemini Trust, which gives families with twins nutritious food, and in various ways supports them till they have found confidence to begin facing life independently.

Gemini helps with children's schooling costs, and gives their parents training in skills which will bring in an income: tailoring, silversmithing, silk screening and spice production. Fikre (her name means 'My Love') has taken in another mother of twins (Zenabech, on the left) whose husband had turned her out, and now they all live together in this hut, along with Fikre's two older children. Fikre has shown the amazing generosity of someone who has herself been given hope.

Mark 12:41-44
She out of her poverty has put in everything she had, all she had to live on. (v44)

February

Conflict and its aftermath

Christian Aid/Nic Dunlop

A prosthetic foot for a landmine victim in Phnom Penh, Cambodia

Cambodia

Hidden landmines

Green fields and water, sun and clouds, cheerful faces – but death beneath their feet, for young and old alike, working or playing. For these are the new 'killing fields' of Cambodia. The rice needs transplanting, but these fields have been mined, and the mines are not visible. They have to be searched out and destroyed, one by one, an expensive, slow and dangerous task, and there are up to eight million of them in Cambodia alone. This is the aftermath of a war in which both sides used mines, and thousands more people, adults and children, are expected to lose limbs or be maimed, well into the 21st century.

The necessary work of reclaiming the farmland, from which most Cambodians earn their living, is held back because of the lasting risk posed by the landmines. Christian Aid supports CIDSE (Coopération Internationale pour le Développement et la Solidarité) and Church World Service and Witness, who help local communities to run their own self-rehabilitation programmes. They also fund the clearing of mines, and retrain those who have lost limbs and other injured people so that they can once more earn their living.

'Landmines react with the same ferocity to the footstep of a child as they do to a soldier. They are primed to kill and maim whether there is war or peace.'

Michael Hawkes, Christian Aid

Christian Aid/Mike Goldwater/Network

God our protector,
watch over us all,
and set our feet on the right path.
Walk with the children
who cannot trust the ground beneath them;
give courage to those
who seek out the hidden danger;
and strengthen the injured
to live and work again.

Ezekiel 34:27
The ground will yield its produce, and my people will live in security on their own soil.

Christian Aid/Paul Lowe/Magnum

O Lord our God,
our help in ages past,
our refuge in time of fear:
bless to us today
the food on our table
and the love in our hearts;
that wherever life takes us,
we may be at home with you.

Huancayo, Peru

Displaced families

The family says grace together over a frugal meal. The room where Martiano Malpica, his wife Adriana and their four children prepare food and eat is just big enough for this table and the fire in the corner. Nearby, the whole family sleeps in two single beds. The house is not theirs, but belongs to a family that has gone elsewhere in search of a better life. For Martiano and Adriana this place is an uncertain refuge. Born and bred high in the Andes, like thousands of others they were driven out by warring guerillas and government forces, leaving their homes, lands, animals and livelihood. Even where they are now, cuts in health, education and local services have forced many out of work.

A local organisation, IDET (the Institute for Democracy and Labour), supports these indigenous campesinos in various ways so that they can once again rely on their own skills and knowledge. Martiano, with others from his community, gets a small loan once or twice a month, which he uses to buy alpaca wool, sheep and cheese to sell for a small profit. In such ways, he and his extended family can retain their dignity and keep some hope for the future for themselves and their children.

'I want my children to be different from me. I want them to have an education and I don't want them to spend their lives weighed down by fear and poverty. We can't go back now, there is nothing left for us to go back to.'

Martiano Malpica

Psalm 9:9-10
The Lord is a stronghold for the oppressed, a stronghold in times of trouble. (v9)

Nuba mountains, Sudan

Survival

'The war has made us all suffer. We need security to live peacefully again. The mountains can give us all we need to live.'

A Nuba man

At first sight this scene from the Nuba mountains, in the Kordofan region of Sudan, is relaxed and peaceful: the graceful figure of a Nuba woman tipping water from a bowl into a water pot. But look closer and you will see that the woman on the left is having to reach down to collect water from a hand-dug well. The deep bore wells from which these people once drew water have been destroyed during the prolonged civil unrest in Sudan. Reliable water supplies were deliberately targeted to control people's freedom of movement.

Many of the Nuba people have been displaced and dispersed, even exiled, and those who remain in this mountainous region cultivate their fields in conditions that are often dangerous, even when the rain is plentiful. Apart from the Catholic Church, the only group working in this difficult area is the Nuba Relief, Rehabilitation and Development Society (NRRDS), a humanitarian organisation staffed by and dedicated to the well-being of the Nuba people. NRRDS seeks ways to improve the water supply and protect it to keep the source clean, so that women do not have to dig wells with their bare hands. Christian Aid supports the efforts of the isolated Nuba people to force survival out of their deep poverty and insecurity.

Christian Aid/Dan Collison

Women fetching water
always look full of grace,
creating an idyllic picture
of rural calm.
This is not leisure, but survival;
so is the graceful posture.
Water must be found,
dug for, lifted, carried far,
and its essential weight
will break the back of those who do it wrong.
God give the women strength
each day to carry survival to their homes.

Psalm 23
Even though I walk through the darkest valley, I fear no evil; for you are with me. (v4)

'We don't have much, but God helps us and we can stand up like human beings. We are able to clothe ourselves. We may not have as much as other people but we are still standing, still surviving.'

Worknesh Kelem

Christian Aid/Adrian Arbib

Northern Ethiopia

Rebuilding lives

The tank is there still, reminder of years of bitter conflict, but it is rusting, and a child props himself against it as he watches the sheep. The lamb signals new life, new enterprise among the hard-pressed communities of this area of northern Ethiopia, on the edge of the Great Rift Valley. It is a land of periodic drought, further hampered by the years of neglect and extensive soil-erosion through removal of trees for firewood, animal fodder and building materials.

The Ethiopian Orthodox Church organises development projects to build terraces to protect farmland from further erosion, to plant trees, and to offer local farmers advice and drought-resistant seeds so that their families can eat more healthily. They also work to improve the water supply, protecting springs and developing irrigation systems. Much-needed additional health facilities and a road-building project to improve access to market are further ways in which the church aims to enable the people of this area to become more self-sufficient in this beautiful but difficult landscape.

God of peace and plenty,
you cherish all that gives life.
May we see our instruments of war
rust with irrelevance,
our children dream their future,
the earth produce its food,
and the people flourish.

Micah 4:1-7
They shall beat their swords into ploughshares, and their spears into pruning hooks. (v3)

March
Women

Christian Aid/Elaine Duigenan

Members of the Farna Women's Group in Ghana bring back the morning's catch of fish to be smoked

Unformed, not women yet,
the small girls wonder
what shape their lives will take,
whether they can choose.
Give them the strength of sisters
to learn, and dream,
and build their growing hope
beyond that narrow sphere
to which the past constrains them.

Christian Aid/ Herriet Logan/Network

Andhra Pradesh,
India

A future for girls

Two faces: reflected in the mirror is Anita's, intent on her 'make up'; in the background her older sister Nassama looks on, apart yet concerned. They are among India's most underprivileged people, both female and dalit (the bottom of the social hierarchy).

Their family lives in a semi-arid area where almost the only occupation available has been working as labourers on others' land for meagre pay. The Deccan Development Society (DDS) works to give women confidence and skills, so that they can make some choices in their lives. Village associations (sangams) have been

started, including the Children's Sangam to which Nassama belongs.

Supported by DDS, Nassama took the huge step of withstanding the extreme disapproval of her family by refusing to marry as a child, and continuing her schooling instead. Her life will still not be at all easy – and will Anita be able to follow in her footsteps even this far? She attends school rather than working as a labourer, thanks to the DDS's help to her family, but she does not belong to the Sangam, and her family is by no means convinced that early marriage is not their best option for her.

'If I do very well at my studies, I would like to become a lawyer because there are so many things going on that are oppressive to women and children.'

Nassama

1 Thessalonians 5:11
Encourage one another and build up each other, as indeed you are doing.

You know about the lives of women –
all those ordinary handmaidens
whose lowliness you have regarded.
Throughout all generations
you will call them blessed,
because they work without resting,
feeding their families,
maintaining their households,
helping each other,
raising chickens and crops and children to your glory.
You will not send them empty away.

This peaceful scene might, you feel, be found anywhere in the world, where women supplement the family food supply with a few hens. But here in Honduras it is a matter of more significance to Maribel Garcia and others like her.

Honduras is burdened by its national debt and the severe economic policies imposed to meet its obligations. Women, who have traditionally been less privileged both at home and in accessing education and opportunities for training, are experiencing even greater hardship than usual at present, especially when they are heads of households. The areas where the Development Association for the Western Region (ADRO) works have a population mainly of indigenous Lenca Indian people. Forty per cent of ADRO's membership is from this group.

ADRO runs a women's programme designed to give women experience in organising themselves to play their part in the regional and national economy – to discover what they can in fact achieve, given encouragement and opportunity. Poultry farming, one way the women participate together, offers improved diet, an additional source of income, and training in administration and marketing.

South-west Honduras

Improving diet

Christian Aid/Wendy Tyndale

'In the Bible it is written that what God gave us is for us all. I often think how beautiful it would be if everyone understood this.'

Women's group, Honduras

Luke 1:46-53
He has filled the hungry with good things. (v53)

Ghana

Running a business

'In the past our children just played on the beach. Now they are in the schools we built.'

Member of the Farna Women's Group

Christian Aid/Elaine Duigenan

Once the fish has been bought from the fishermen, members of the Farna ('by the river') Women's Group must sort it before it is smoked.

Women in rural Ghana play the major role in providing for their families and for this they need some income. With grants from the Freedom from Hunger Campaign (FFHC), women in Chokomey village have developed their own very successful fish-smoking business. They buy the fish from the boats when it is in abundance and smoke it in stoves on wooden racks with handles. These racks have been introduced by FFHC, to help the women avoid burning their hands, and to ensure the fish are smoked evenly. The smoked fish is then taken to the market at Accra, about nine miles away, to be sold.

Despite problems of fluctuating market prices and having to find other small industries in the slack fishing season, the women of the village not only repay their annual revolving loans, but have used profits to build first a nursery school and then a primary school, both of which now have teachers supplied by the government. It is a proud achievement for the Farna Women's Group, and one that has already inspired another village to build a school for its children.

The women get down to work
gathering the sea's harvest.
Each step must be done with care,
each woman sure of her task.
It is for the children:
food in their mouths,
clothes for their backs,
schools to learn in.
God give these determined women
the future they deserve.

Proverbs 31:13-31 Give her a share in the fruit of her hands,
and let her works praise her in the city gates. (v31)

Rwanda

Coping as widows

This woman is a widow of genocide. Revealing her own name or publishing her particular tragedy might still endanger her life. So what follows is the typical story of someone whom we will call 'Françoise'.

Like thousands of other women in Rwanda, Françoise is a survivor of massacre – her husband murdered months before their first child was born, her extended family dispersed or killed, some of the killers being her former friends and neighbours. Françoise lives by buying vegetables to resell outside her door.

But 'her door' means little: she has only the ruins of a home, and she has found shelter of a kind in the houses of others who fled from the massacre. Many of them have now returned, so more than once she has been given a fortnight to move on. She has, however, begun to find support and friendship in AVEGA (Association des veuves du génocide d'avril 1994), set up by widows themselves, supporting each other after their horrific experiences. Christian Aid supports AVEGA's work to assist widows in greatest need to rebuild their homes, or build new homes in settlements with other widows (women are now 70 per cent of Rwanda's population), and to plan and run agricultural co-operatives and other projects.

'The people who killed have gained nothing. Doing bad things will not help solve anything. The only way forward is to do good.'

A widow who was a founding member of AVEGA

Christian Aid/Anthony Swift

So many women
across the ages
have looked on horror,
seen their men slain,
wept until they have no more tears,
and then had to live.
God give them again
the wish to embrace life;
may they turn to each other
and be made strong,
that death may have no more dominion.

Matthew 27:55-56 Many women were also there [when Jesus was crucified], looking on from a distance. (v55)

Crispin Hughes

April

Building communities

John Majok, a pastor in a refugee camp in the Sudan, moulded this cross into the wall of his hut

Diakonia Council of Churches

KwaZulu-Natal,
South Africa

Seeking reconciliation

Jesus our saviour,
your heart was broken
by the world's agony;
you carried the pain
we make each other bear.
Remember those who carry
the difficult work of peace,
bearing the cost of memory,
seeking detailed justice,
facing day by day
the hard recurring choice
whether to ask forgiveness,
whether to forgive.

'Advocacy is part of a very old biblical tradition of standing up on behalf of those treated unjustly.'

Article in *Inselelo*, Diakonia Council of Churches Newsletter

One's first thought may be 'What strength is here! And what devotion!' But this is also the face of endurance and of suffering. Here in the ecumenical Good Friday march through Durban, South African churches bear witness to the Cross in a society that still has a long and painful task ahead.

The Diakonia Council of Churches (DCC) is based in an area of KwaZulu-Natal where there is enormous deprivation, and where violence and instability have even increased since South Africa's democratic elections in 1994. Among its priorities are peacemaking and peace-building: it helps member churches to reflect theologically on the root causes of the violence, to work with or provide alternative peace structures, to facilitate dialogue between conflicting groups, and to assist traumatised survivors.

The DCC also helps the churches to prepare people for full and active participation in democratic society, and to learn how to 'push the appropriate people for change'; to reflect and act effectively on economic issues, and on the health and social crisis produced by the rising number of people with AIDS. The Good Friday march allows those who have been involved in terrible wrongs, whether as victims or as perpetrators, to seek reconciliation through the Cross.

Luke 19:41-42 As Jesus came near and saw the city, he wept over it, saying, 'If you, even you, had only recognised on this day the things that make for peace!'

Dominican Republic

Honour and respect

Christian Aid/Katty Isles

When honour or respect
are not daily what greets me;
when my work is unvalued,
my needs dismissed,
or my voice unheard,
teach me my dignity.
For with you, O Lord, I have confidence,
and in your presence
I shall never be put to shame.

Siana is clearly a woman of spirit – and she needs to be, as a Haitian migrant worker in the Dominican Republic. The Haitian population, mainly of African descent, is looked down on by the Spanish-speaking Dominicans. Life is hard for the migrant workers, who are often without legal rights, and subject to victimisation. Onè Respé is a group set up to empower women in this situation. Its name recalls the gracious courtesy of Haitian country culture: 'Onè!' (honour) is said by a guest asking to enter the house; 'Respé!' (respect) is the welcoming response.

In and round Santiago (northern Dominican Republic), Onè Respé has started a 'Little School' for some of the children of Haitian single mothers. They also work with mixed women's groups, aiming to increase understanding and respect between the two communities, so that women learn to participate fully in the decisions that shape their lives, and work co-operatively on community problems. A key method used by Onè Respé is community Bible study. Each week a Bible passage is discussed by the women, who apply it to the practical issues they are facing together. Then they pray about them.

'I really am a person – doing the Bible study gave me my dignity as a woman. I feel very much loved by God, and as such I can help to create a better community.'

Chaki del Carmen Abreu, community worker with Onè Respé

Christian Aid/Harriet Logan/Network

'We solve problems
without force.
Our best weapon
is our tongue.'

**Ramón Andrade,
peace commission
co-ordinator**

O Lord, teach me to be strong,
to disarm those who threaten,
to turn away anger
with a gentle word,
to refuse to let past conflicts
control the future,
to find your new way
where force no longer rules,
but generosity.

Nicaragua

Disarming former combatants

A man at prayer: children sit quietly by, and others move about in this village church in the Nicaraguan countryside. All looks peaceful enough, yet great burdens weigh on these people: not only do they struggle with the business of feeding themselves and their families with very few resources, but much of their countryside is in a state of anarchy.

Although the civil war ended years ago, former combatants from both sides threaten any economic revival and real peace. Frustrated at being unable to reinsert themselves adequately into society, they use their weapons to pressure the government by blocking roads and taking towns, and survive by resorting to banditry. During the war waged by US-backed rebels (known as contra-revolutionaries/ 'contras' or 'freedom-fighters', depending on your allegiance) against the Sandinista government, peace commissions were set up in areas of particular conflict by Nicaragua's most important aid and relief organisation, the Council of Evangelical Churches (CEPAD). Along with the Catholic Church, they continue the difficult and dangerous work of reintegrating combatants into often very tiny communities, where the war caused profound and bitter divisions. Prayer and Bible study form part of CEPAD's training programme for local volunteers. They learn to use negotiation and hospitality to persuade the bandits to give up their arms.

Matthew 5:38-48
I say to you, Love your enemies and pray for those who persecute you. (v44)

'We want people in Malawi to have power through democracy by 2009 but this requires us all to take action so that this vision is not just a dream.'

Robert Phiri, PAC

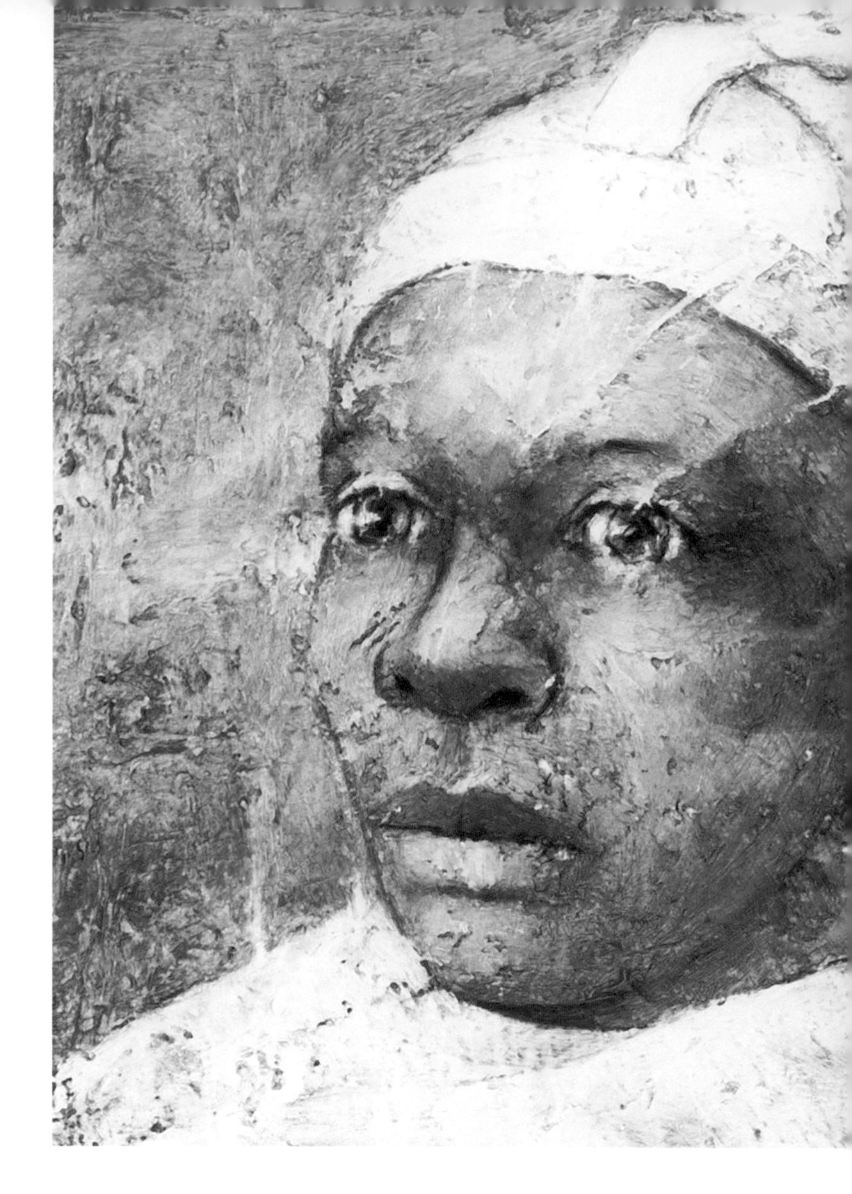

Malawi

Hopes and fears

Illustration/photo: 'Head', painting, acrylic on cotton, Peter White

When I am afraid to speak
because I feel ignorant,
Lord, let me find my voice.
When I fear to trust others
because they are different,
or because they have power,
Lord, give me courage.
When I feel manipulated,
and I do not know how to argue my case,
Lord, help me to choose well.

The artist has caught in this woman's face the huge and real fears that surround Malawians at this stage in the life of their country – one of the world's poorest, and struggling, amidst severe economic hardship, to meet the demands of the recent changeover to a multi-party form of government. Civic education programmes are urgently needed, made harder by the fact that most Malawians are illiterate, and live in remote rural areas.

The Public Affairs Committee (PAC) played a significant role in the transition from a one-party state. Basically a religious organisation of Protestants, Catholics and Muslims, it now works hard to educate people to take part in democratic processes. There is a small core staff, and many volunteers who carry out much of the educational work, training religious leaders and local politicians at district level to develop democratic processes. Many politicians hinder this work, carrying over vote-buying, intimidation and violence from the old regime. Ordinary people, not least women, few of whom up till now have been active in public life, can learn from PAC how to take up their responsibilities and play their part in the new democracy.

Deuteronomy 30:19-20
Choose life so that you and your descendants may live. (v19)

afédirect

May

Supporters in the United Kingdom and Ireland

Eildon Dyer

Wilma Murray and Kathleen Smyrl of Milngavie Christian Aid Committee (near Glasgow) with a catering pack of fairly traded coffee

Christian Aid/Jeff Williams

Let me find it in me
to give my money
as I do my hospitality –
courteously:
wanting to treat my guests
to the best I can afford,
finding pleasure in providing,
hoping to build up friendship;
learning to give as God gives,
with all my heart.

Fundraising

There is always a Christian Aid stall at the Urdd National Youth Eisteddfod in Wales, and volunteers try to raise funds in a way that captures the imagination of passers-by. Here, Gareth offers his services as a shoeshine boy, in honour of Moti in India who does this daily in order that his family may eat (see p18).

This is part of the huge annual fundraising effort around Christian Aid Week, in which more than 300,000 volunteers – usually churchgoers – take part, raising overall about £10 million. Many local events are organised, like book sales, auctions and sponsored walks.

But the major exercise, carefully planned by local committee organisers and by Christian Aid representatives in churches, is recruiting collectors to go round the streets with the familiar red envelope to ask for donations from every household.

Asking is not easy for many people. Sometimes there is an unfriendly response on the doorstep. But there are always those (not necessarily the well off) who are startlingly generous. And it is the largest joint activity the churches undertake together each year – an act of witness showing the local community that the church cares about the world.

'Do you mean to say that in Christian Aid Week, respectable church people in your country go out onto the streets to beg on behalf of the world's poor?'

Comment from Santiago, Chile

Luke 6:20-38 Give, and it will be given to you. A good measure, pressed down, shaken together, running over, will be put into your lap. (v38)

Praying

'History belongs to the intercessors, who believe the future into being... Hope imagines its future, and then acts as if that future is irresistible.'

Walter Wink,
Engaging the Powers,
Fortress 1992

In 1996, Westminster Abbey was host to a special *Songs of Praise* for Christian Aid Week. Each year in the second week of May, thousands of churches across the United Kingdom and Ireland celebrate their connection with all who are poor and excluded in this world. They do this, not only by collecting money from their local community, but also through worship.

Often different congregations will join together for Sunday morning worship. But in any case, churches are encouraged by knowing that so many others are praying with them on the same theme. Through the power of prayer we can learn to bear one another's burdens.

Prayer is not a passive alternative to 'doing something' in the cause of justice. It provides the life-blood, the energy and the sure direction underlying the work we engage in. Without prayer it is easy to burn out and despair. Prayer expresses our longing for the kind of world we do not yet see, where, in the words of Christian Aid's statement of commitment, 'all shall be included in the feast of life'.

Christian Aid/Jeremy Hartley

O God,
you took upon you
the yoke of humanity
and the burden of love,
and did not find it easy;
let us learn from you
to share the weight
of all this aching world,
that our souls may be light,
our hearts rested,
as together we are carried by you
in Jesus Christ.

Matthew 11:28-30 Take my yoke upon you... and you will find rest for your souls.
For my yoke is easy, and my burden is light. (v29-30)

'Knowledge emerges
only through
invention and
re-invention,
through restless,
impatient, continuing,
hopeful enquiry...
in the world, with
the world, and
with each other.'

Paolo Freire, *Pedagogy of the Oppressed*, Penguin 1972

Christian Aid/Renzo Frontoni

O God,
Let me learn like a child,
absorbed in your word,
in touch with the detail
of this your interesting world.
Let me taste the variety
of people and place,
comfortable with myself,
seeking new friends,
expecting, daily, to grow.

Learning

Lucy takes care to get it right making her first samosas, at an event organised in Church Stretton, Shropshire, to celebrate Christian Aid Week 1997. India was the focus, and the idea was not just to raise money, but to learn in a 'hands-on' way what it means to live in a different culture – even what the food tastes like.

Children are growing up into a world which increasingly is connected by sophisticated communications systems, but still relentlessly divided in terms of wealth, opportunity, and access to skills and resources. It is important that young and old have the chance to learn about the ordinary lives of those whom they will never meet face to face. It helps to step into the shoes of another, and to realise that, however different the details of daily life, some of the issues and problems we face are similar.

Christian Aid resources teachers with classroom materials that bring the world closer – packs, videos and practical learning ideas. Area staff and volunteers across the United Kingdom and Ireland raise awareness by preaching, running workshops and meetings, and by introducing people to visitors from the overseas programmes we support. Hearing the story direct from those who do the work is one of the most powerful ways of learning to see the world differently.

Matthew 13:3-23
Let anyone with ears listen! (v9)

'Off Your Trolley' was a youth initiative in the Irish Republic, linked to Christian Aid's fair trade challenge to supermarkets. Hundreds of young people marched with their teachers during One World Week 1997, and, outside Leinster House in Dublin, presented Senator Fergal Quinn with a packet of fairly traded tea and a campaign pack. He is the owner of the Superquin chain of stores and has promised to hammer out with the other supermarkets in the Republic of Ireland a code of practice for ethical trading, seeking to ensure fair wages and safe conditions for those who harvest the produce which ends up on our shelves.

The reasons why people remain trapped in poverty are often global rather than local. Another major campaign concerns the unpayable foreign debts which paralyse the economies of poor nations and cause their people to suffer great hardship.

Biblical principles set limits to the rights of creditors to pursue the very poor for debts they cannot pay. Christian Aid supporters, along with others, are putting pressure on decision-makers to find ways of remitting the debt of the world's 50 poorest countries as we move into a new millennium. Each person alone may be helpless to change the way of the world, but acting together can make a difference.

O God, you promise a world
where those who now weep shall laugh;
those who are hungry shall feast;
those who are poor now, and excluded,
shall have your kingdom for their own.
I want this world too.
I renounce despair.
I will act for change.
I choose to be included
in your great feast of life.

Christian Aid/Michael Begg

Campaigning

'Thank God for people who do not have hearts of stone.'

Don Enrique, Nicaragua, of people willing to campaign

James 2:14-17 If a brother or sister is naked and lacks daily food... and yet you do not supply their bodily needs, what is the good of that? (v16)

Christian Aid/Harriet Logan/Network

June

Food security

A seedling is planted in a tree nursery in India

Let us bless the Lord,
who has not given all places
the same ground,
or all plants the same growth:
for seeds that know their soil,
poor as it is;
for fruits that can flourish
where they best belong;
for the harvest that can be gathered
around a settled home.

Christian Aid/Michael Begg

West Bengal, India

Growing your own

'I have learned a great deal about vegetable growing. Service Centre has taught us to eat nutritionally and grow vegetables in an organic way. We now have enough to feed the family and soon we will be able to generate an income by selling our vegetables in the market.'

Village woman

Every gardener will warm to this scene, with its well-trodden path leading past the family garden to the pumpkin plants trailing over the thatched roof – and most of all, the sense that things are being grown here, carefully tended for a family's use and well-being. Yet it is a new venture in this part of India, or at least a revival and development of older ways: farming methods of recent times have increasingly degraded the soil and made seasonal migration necessary for villagers who could not earn enough to feed themselves without leaving home for several months every year.

The movement towards sustainable agriculture is being spearheaded by the Development Research Communication and Services Centre (DRCSC), popularly known as Service Centre, based in Calcutta. Its Sustainable Agriculture Network helps field groups, by such methods as running workshops, supplying seeds, and using street theatre to highlight new or more appropriate farming methods. In such ways villagers learn how to supply their own basic food needs and share their new skills without having to leave home every year. Seeds of indigenous fruits and pulses are sought out and supplied, along with wild and local varieties of chillies and vegetables, and suitable plant seeds from elsewhere.

Psalm 67:6-7
The earth has yielded its increase; God, our God, has blessed us. (v6)

Galaha, Sri Lanka

Natural fertilisers

You may prefer your compost heaps decently screened at the bottom of your garden, but here at the Gami Seva Sevana (GSS) centre they are proudly displayed. Local people can visit the 16-acre model farm for short or longer training courses, learning a wide range of skills.

In the early 1970s unproductive tea estates were broken up and small portions of land allotted to local people, children of those who had formerly laboured there. But the hill-slopes are subject to erosion and the soil now low-yielding. When, under World Bank pressure, fertiliser subsidies were removed in 1992, people found themselves unable to support their families. GSS is one of the few agencies in Sri Lanka trying to address this: the farm's interdependent units, run on organic principles, allow soil enrichment through animal dung added to the weeds and food waste in compost heaps.

Families who have learned better farming methods from GSS may now own a couple of cows (and be part of a milk-producers' co-operative), chickens, goats or rabbits, and grow a great variety of foodstuffs; they may even be able to save for their children's education. Like compost, GSS is making a difference.

O God,
with whom nothing is lost, nothing is wasted,
we thank you for the miracle of compost –
our daily leavings, what we throw away,
able, with time and care,
to fertilise the earth.
Take what we regard as useless in our lives,
failure, pain or poverty,
and transform them through your power
to become a rich source of growth.

Christian Aid/DK Crevance

'When we import seeds of vegetables, such as carrots or leeks, they come from transnational corporations and have... been designed to respond to fertiliser. So there's a need for local production of seed that is suitable for organic agriculture.'

Ranjith de Silva, a founder of GSS

Mark 4:30-32 The mustard seed is the smallest of all the seeds on earth; yet when it is sown it grows up and becomes the greatest of all shrubs. (v31-32)

O God whose heart
is rooted in our earth,
give us minds to question
the practices that harm it.
Show us the detailed threads
linking life to life,
and make our hands delicate
to tend our plants with care.

Christian Aid/Tricia Spanner

Edson Mashudhu questions the modern farming methods he was taught at school. He now teaches some of the traditional techniques, learnt from his father, in his work for Silveira House agricultural training centre.

Small-scale farming faces many problems in Zimbabwe: crowded communal lands, poor-quality soil, erratic rainfall, over-grazing and over-cultivation. The cost of artificial fertilisers is so high that they are beyond the reach of poorer farmers.

Silveira House is working to give rural families an alternative that will enable them to grow enough food to feed themselves. It works with poor farmers in Mutoko district, training them to use the natural elements around them in an environmentally friendly farming method called permaculture.

At Silveira House there is a garden demonstrating permaculture techniques. The garden is planted in concentric circles and food crops are carefully mixed with herbs, green manures, medicinal plants and those that repel insects. Once a garden is established there is no need to use expensive pesticides and a family can grow enough food to eat.

Mutoko district, Zimbabwe

Environment-friendly farming

'In permaculture we work with nature, not against it. We encourage chameleons, along with bees, wasps and other insects, to do various jobs for us rather than using chemicals, etc.'

Edson Mashudhu

Job 12:7-10
Ask the plants of the earth, and they will teach you. (v8)

O God, we give you thanks
for all the natural wealth
of your industrious creation:
the trees' protective shade,
the complex life of insects,
harnessed to work in harmony
with human needs.
May we welcome and use what they offer,
without exploiting it,
keeping the food store safe
for future generations.

The Gambia

Income to buy food

There are two ways of making sure you have enough food – you grow it or you buy it. In the Gambia, villagers experience a 'hungry season' of about three months when their stored harvest has run out. That is when they need an income, and these beehives hanging from the trees can provide one.

The Gambia is a predominantly agricultural country, but despite this it cannot grow all the food it needs and thus relies on having to import what it cannot produce.

Poverty in the Gambia is most noticeable in rural areas. GARDA (Gambia Rural Development Agency) works with village communities, and is responsible for encouraging self-sufficiency through a variety of projects, including traditional bee-keeping. Although the baskets are beautiful, GARDA is now introducing modern, free-standing wooden hives, which are easier to empty and can hold more honeycombs.

Most of the bee-keeping and honey-making work is done by women, who are also planting fruit trees to attract the bees. In the village of Malik Nana, for example, there are 15 hives – supplied as a loan by GARDA – which are harvested twice a year. The women keep some of the honey and sell the rest.

Christian Aid/Clare Parkes

'GARDA is the first agency to come to this area; they have enabled the women of the village to earn money on their own.'

Mrs Awan Dao, President of the Women's Group in Malik Nana

Psalm 81
With honey from the rock I would satisfy you. (v16)

Christian Aid/Elaine Duigenan

July

Water

In Marala village in Tanzania, women who used to have to walk three miles to collect water can now use this tap on their doorsteps

The Dogon people are described by other Malians as the people 'not scared of work', and it is not hard to see why.

They live on the Dogon Plateau in northern central Mali: it is 50 miles wide and 130 miles north to south. It is dry, very hot and made of bedrock. Growing anything here involves real ingenuity and sheer hard work. Severe droughts in the 1970s and 1980s forced many of the Dogon people to leave, but those who have stayed, with a little help from outside, have managed not only to go on growing vegetables but also to grow a cash crop of onions in little patches of soil edged with stones.

Water has been a major problem, with successive droughts and the advance of the Sahara desert hitting traditional water sources. Now the Catholic Mission of Bandiagara is sinking new wells, like this one at Dansongo village, blasting through the hard rock to find clean water. Not only do crops benefit, but there are now far fewer cases of diarrhoea, parasites and the painful guinea-worm. People here still leave for work in the towns in the dry season, but these days they come back again when it is over.

The Dogon Plateau, Mali

Sinking wells

Come to the waters,
all you who are thirsty:
children who need water
free from diseases,
women who need respite
from labour and searching,
plants that need moisture
rooted near the bedrock,
find here a living spring.
O God, may we thirst
for your waters of justice,
and learn to deny no one
the water of life.

Christian Aid/Mike Goldwater/Network

'Before we got the new well, our water was muddy, tasted nasty and made us ill. With this new well the water is good and our children no longer suffer so much from diarrhoea and swollen tummies.'

Fanta Kassogue, Dogon Plateau

Isaiah 55 Ho, everyone who thirsts, come to the waters; and you that have no money, come, buy and eat! (v1)

Potosí, Bolivia

Demanding clean water

Long before 29 August 1996, the *campesinos* of this mountainous and very poor region of Latin America's poorest country struggled with the ill effects on their lives of large-scale mining operations nearby. The serious landslip of that day ruptured a dam and brought 10,000 tonnes of mining effluent into the River Caiza and other tributaries. The resulting water pollution, so clearly visible in this picture, affected a wide area and about 10,000 people plus their animals and crops. Causananchispaj ('To be able to live') is a Potosí-based organisation set up in 1991 to help a number of *ayllus* (traditional community groupings of settlements) to work together to improve their standards of health and living. Although the mining company accepted some liability, it was only with the action of Causananchispaj, together with the people of these communities (with whom they were already working), that materials needed to procure an alternative water supply were offered. With the financial help of CAFOD and of Christian Aid, who also lobbied on behalf of Causananchispaj, and the labour supplied by local people, clean water was largely assured in this small area at least. In the face of seemingly overwhelming obstacles, some degree of success was achieved because people were enabled to identify and fight for their rights.

Careless who drinks,
they have embittered
the sweet waters of life.
Let justice roll down like fountains,
and righteousness
like a mighty stream.

Christian Aid/Judith Escribano

'To know Potosí is to know the history of Latin America, since it was from here that fortunes were made and mass exploitation occurred. Much of the investment from mining goes abroad; while local workers continue to die in their hundreds each year.'

Crisológo Alemán, Director of Causananchispaj

Isaiah 41:17-20 When the poor and needy seek water, and there is none, and their tongue is parched with thirst, I the Lord will answer them. (v17)

'Now we have water, clean toilets and playgroups for the children. But the most important changes are the changes within the people.'

Rukmani, member of Sorag village committee

Christian Aid/Michael Begg

The Himalayas, India

Saving women's time

A simple tap.
Water that is reliable, clean, there.
O God, whenever I drink
or clean my teeth, or take a bath,
water the garden,
wash vegetables or clothes,
remind me to give thanks,
wholeheartedly,
for the freedom that surrounds me –
and I hardly notice it.

Two generations of women in Sorag village liberated by a tap! The woman can wash her vegetables conveniently; the girl, who has just cleaned her teeth at the tap, is off to school. With water so close to home, she will have more time for reading.

Getting clean water in the Himalayas has got harder and harder. With the loss of trees and topsoil (through mining, logging and construction), water quickly pours down the steep rocky slopes, and women are forced to use distant heavily polluted water holes. Their children become ill and many have died from water-borne diseases.

The Kassar Trust was founded in 1986. It started to help village communities to build simple wells, training villagers to take over the work. Using cheap technology, underground streams are detected and dug out. They are then surrounded by a brick wall to protect the stream and topped with a hand-pump.

In addition to saving women's time and effort in water collection and overcoming health problems, the wells led to the formation of village committees which have moved on to other projects. Sorag itself has started a balwadi (playgroup), which brings together not only children but their parents as well.

Isaiah 58:10-12 The Lord will... satisfy your needs in parched places, and make your bones strong; and you shall be like a watered garden. (v11)

‘Since visiting Mozambique with Christian Aid, “spring water” has taken on a whole new meaning for me... The next time you have a bottle of spring water, think of the people of Namarroi.’

Eildon Dyer, Christian Aid

Namarroi, Mozambique

Bringing the water to town

Let us bless the Lord
for strong communities,
battered by war,
deprived of the basics,
but connected by courage and hard work,
determined to live.
Let us celebrate those who had nothing,
but put their backs into it
to renew their water,
to renew their health,
to renew their children’s hope.

Christian Aid/Steve Lewis

You may still have to wait to fill your bucket in Namarroi, but the water will be clean and crystal clear because it comes from a spring, and you won't have to carry it far home.

Namarroi is a very isolated town and was hard hit by the civil war when its electricity and water systems were destroyed. All the water for the little hospital with its maternity wing had to be carried uphill on people's heads. None of the attempts to pump water from the lake were successful and instead it was decided to bring water from a mountain waterfall about three miles away through the bush.

The Christian Council of Mozambique provided help in the form of engineering advice and funding, but local people dug the trenches and dammed the waterfall by building a retaining wall of broken-up rocks held together by cement that had to be carried, on heads again, through the bush and over terrain too rough even for wheelbarrows. It was a huge effort to build, but once the gravity system was in place it could be maintained by a local group, who also give out information about good sanitation and hygiene practices.

Psalm 72:1-4
May the mountains yield prosperity for the people. (v3)

August
Small enterprise loans

Christian Aid/DK Crevance

In K Parraipatti quarry, Tamil Nadu, India, members of the local village association now own the leasehold on the business

'Usually when we do the washing the whole family is involved and we sing songs as we wash.'

Periakaruppan, dhobi

Christian Aid/DK Crevance

More work choices

There are 13 dhobi (washerfolk) families in Suliochanapatti village who between them wash and iron the clothes of some 1,500 families. Traditionally their caste makes this their only possible occupation.

The whole process of collecting the items of clothing on donkeys, sorting, washing, rinsing, drying, ironing, packing and redistributing will take 14 days and will be done twice a month.

Because of the expectations of their low caste, the dhobis were not only very poorly paid by the villagers, but were stuck in the only occupation allowed to them. In 1990, SIRD (the Society for Integrated Rural Development) organised these families into a sangam (association), which enabled them to join together to press for higher wages. It also established a common fund, so that each sangam member began to pay a regular subscription, and could take out loans. Through this credit scheme, dhobis have been able to buy goats, pigs, donkeys and cows, to add small-scale farming to their traditional work. Some have even bought agricultural land.

By achieving better working conditions, and finding they have a choice of occupation, the dhobi families have become more confident and respected in their community.

Christ our Lord,
who took a towel, bent down,
and wiped the feet of your friends,
wash our hearts also.
Remember the invisible ones
who keep our world clean:
clothes, homes, offices, streets.
May we not despise this work
which serves our self-respect,
and keep no one trapped in poverty
doing our dirty work.

Matthew 23:11-12
The greatest among you will be your servant. (v11)

'The best way to assist our women is to help them stand on their own two feet.'

Pastor John Bangonluri, Co-ordinator of the Kaleo Suntaa women's project

Upper West Region, Ghana

'Self-help'

You need strong arms to process sheanuts. They are pounded twice: once after peeling off the soft outer layer and then again after the pounded kernels have been fried. The semi-liquid paste is then hand mixed with water until a liquid paste can be heated, allowed to cool and the oil skimmed off the top. What is left is made into small round portions ready for sale and used for cooking or skin cream.

The women in the picture belong to Chaangu Women's Group, one of the 11 village groups in the Upper West Region of Ghana that are part of the Kaleo Suntaa Baptist Women's Development Project. The region itself is one of the poorest in Ghana. Many men have left the area in search of work elsewhere, leaving women to bear sole responsibility for the family.

Suntaa means 'self-help': the project offers the women's groups loans to start or improve small businesses. For the women who process sheanuts, this means that they can buy more raw materials, and having organised as a group they have become known by local traders, which saves them the worry of getting their product to market.

Christian Aid/Elaine Duigenan

Without technology,
each part of the process
takes skill, timing, stamina,
and sheer physical strength.
Arms, back and shoulders
ache with the effort.
God give these women sometimes
the space to rest;
and make their work count.

Ecclesiasticus 38:27-34
All these rely on their hands, and are skilful in their own work. (v31)

When a heavy animal like a water buffalo gets sick, the vet has to come to her. Fortunately, shortly after Dodong gave her this antibiotic injection, the heifer revived and was able to get on her feet again.

Water buffaloes provide the muscle power on farms in this part of the Philippines, so their health is crucial. Without a traction animal, farmers have to plough and transport produce by hand and this punishing work takes far longer to do. Small farmers cannot afford to buy their own animals, so MuCARD (Muslim Christian Action for Rural Development) gives them a loan. MuCARD is a large organisation which includes many credit schemes to help people improve their farming or their small business. Sometimes, instead of a cash investment, MuCARD distributes heifer water buffaloes to farmers' groups, who share the use of the animal for heavy farming tasks. Because maintaining their health is so important, MuCARD workers like Dodong can be called on for emergency veterinary treatment.

Water buffaloes not only do the work of many people, but can obviously produce offspring. When a calf is born, it is given back to the programme to be loaned on to another group of farmers, to help them to get back on their feet.

Creator God,
who made both great and small,
we thank you for the animals
who share our lives,
labour for us and feed us,
provide company and protection.
May we treat them with care,
respecting all of life that you have given.

Christian Aid/Jo Elms

Using animals on the farm

'The animal looked as if she was going to die. But they gave her several shots of antibiotic and slowly she revived and got to her feet. Everyone was very happy.'

Jo Elms, Christian Aid staff member visiting the programme

Genesis 2:19 Out of the ground the Lord God formed every animal of the field and every bird of the air, and brought them to the man.

O Lord,
when I cannot manage my life,
when I have taken a wrong course,
when there is no one to support me,
do not leave me in despair.
Remember me, uphold me,
show me the path of life;
give me a new start.

Christian Aid/Gillian Weeks

'I'm very happy. I know everything now. I've learnt how to survive.'

Rose Adubango, 29, who went to Port Bell after a year in Tororo Prison

Another satisfied customer!

Jessica Nansubuga sells many things – charcoal, cassava chips, bananas, woven mats she has made. She rents her stall – four wooden uprights and a roof – and goes early to market to buy supplies. The rent is 5,000 shillings a month. If she splits the charcoal she buys into small bits she can make 1,200 profit on top of this.

Jessica has spent time in prison and her future would have looked bleak if it hadn't been for the National Association of Women's Organisations in Uganda (NAWOU), who launched the Port Bell Women's Resettlement Project in 1995. The first project of its kind in Uganda, it gives women released from prison a new start in life. The women complete a four-month intensive training course, which aims to build their confidence and self-esteem as well as teaching them practical skills like baking, weaving and cattle management.

At the end of the course each woman is given a loan of between 50 and 350 dollars to set up a small business – like Jessica's stall. Out of 80 women helped, only one has returned to prison, and she visited the project after a month to apologise.

Kampala area, Uganda

Making a new start

Psalm 25

Let me not be put to shame, for in you I find refuge. (v20)

September

Emergencies

Christian Aid/Glynn Griffiths

Ali Dulo, near his home in Rhoka village, Kenya. Unusually prolonged rains due to the El Niño effect caused floods in 1998.

When 60-year-old Aung Ma Chin returned from the cyclone shelter on the morning of 20 May 1997 she found her home in ruins.

It had all started the day before. At about 10 o'clock in the morning the wind had begun to blow hard and it started to rain. Volunteers from the Christian Commission for Development in Bangladesh (CCDB), trained in disaster preparedness, started to urge the villagers to move into the specially built cyclone shelter.

When the wind turned violent at about 2pm, Aung Ma Chin went to the shelter with her children and grandchildren, taking with her their valuables and the supplies of dry food they kept ready. They joined the 500 women and children already there, more arriving by the second; the men would come at the last minute.

Winds gusted at 150 miles per hour, pounding the coastline, and left 100 people dead. When a similar cyclone hit Bangladesh in 1991, nearly 140,000 people died. This time, although there were many casualties, thousands of lives were saved by the CCDB's Disaster Preparedness Programme.

Aung Ma Chin knows that when she makes a new house, that too may be devastated some day. But she has life, and she *will* have a new home.

Charles S Sarkar/CCDB

O compassionate Lord,
I would prefer power over the storm,
a secure home,
a life protected from the winds.
But help me to live with storms,
shelter with friends,
see my plans broken,
but not my life;
rebuild again and again from the earth.

'By coming to this centre a lot of our lives have been saved. I am one of them.'

Bina, a villager from the low-lying island of Moheskhali, one of the areas worst hit by the cyclone

Cox's Bazar District, Bangladesh

Preparing for cyclones

Psalm 55:4-8
I would hurry to find a shelter for myself from the raging wind and tempest. (v8)

'O God
Our suffering sigh in heaven is heard
and faith in you will ease all pain.
We shall not give up!'

Gershon Anderson, Sierra Leone

Christian Aid/Helen Atkinson

Sierra Leone

Seed distribution

When the sacks of seeds arrive, the welcoming smiles replace the anxiety, frustration and fear of a people recovering from civil war and military coup.

Sixty-five per cent of the population of Sierra Leone, one of the poorest countries in the world, are small farmers growing rice, cocoa and coffee. Many of them were forced to leave their land during the five-year civil war which ended with democratic elections in February 1996.

Mariana Muyaba's experience is typical: when she returned to her very productive two and a half acres of gently sloping ground, she found it reclaimed by the bush, with trees, shrubs and weeds covering the previously cultivated land.

She registered as a farmer who needed help to restore her farm and received tools, seeds and plants from the Council of Churches of Sierra Leone (CCSL). It took a lot of hard work to prepare the ground, but she, like many other farmers in Sierra Leone, was able to plant her seeds before the military coup of 25 May 1997.

Although the coup again threatened people's security, because the seeds were planted in time, the farmers are now discussing the best ways to work together to store their crops safely to provide seeds for next season.

Though what is past
may be full of loss,
and the present insecure,
never shall despair
take away our future.
Give us the seeds of hope, O God,
and we will clear the ground,
plant and weed and work and laugh,
our harvest safe in your hands.

Genesis 8:22 As long as the earth endures, seedtime and harvest, cold and heat, summer and winter, day and night, shall not cease.

Thai/Burmese border

Refugees

The blank faces of these men, all of them from one or other of Burma's ethnic minority groups, do not conceal their strain, weariness and apprehension. Life at home has become so intolerable that they have made the dangerous journey over the mountains to cross the border into Thailand. They find refuge of a sort in camps just inside the border, and by March 1998 there were approximately 116,000 of them, with reports of many more on the move.

As the Thai government did not officially recognise their refugee status, no official assistance was being provided at that time. Much, however, depends on the Burmese Border Consortium, a group of non-governmental organisations who pool their resources to provide basic food and necessities to the refugees. Some have been forced out of their homes through compulsory relocation; others were unable to endure the conditions of forced labour imposed on them by national government troops who made them 'porter', carrying weapons, or the taxes exacted in lieu of labour. Burmese raids sometimes force refugees to move on, even to return home. The camps are crowded, and offer little scope for self-help. Only the children play happily, while their elders wait, with or without hope.

Lord of compassion,
it is so hard to feel useless,
to be unable to escape from difficulties,
to be dependent on the will of others,
to have no control.
When there is nothing I can do
to decide the future,
give me the power to wait:
to wait without anger,
to wait without tiring of my life.

Christian Aid/Mike Goldwater/Network

'I left in the end because I had to hide in the fields from the military so many times. We hid so they wouldn't take us portering. It was also costing the villages too much to pay them so they wouldn't come back. It really troubled me so I just had to leave. My two brothers came too. My sisters were sad but they're used to it now.'

Young male refugee

Matthew 8:20
The Son of man has nowhere to lay his head.

‘Since Egyptian times, seven years of good harvest have always been followed by a poor year, so we have always carried out emergency-prevention programmes in the communities. We think this is much better than implementing emergency programmes once the disaster occurs, since these merely engender dependency.’

Juan Vargas, Co-ordinator, CIPE

Judith Escribano

Bolivia

Preparing for drought

It is easy to see that at the time this photo was taken (November 1997) this part of Bolivia, in the high Andes, was very dry. Periods without rainfall, though common enough in this, one of the poorest parts of the country, can intensify into drought conditions, especially during 'El Niño', a disturbance in the world's normal climate which occurs about every seven years. The people have sometimes been driven to seek work elsewhere in order to support their families. CIPE (Centre for Educational Advance and Research) aims to encourage them to make the most out of the rainfall their land does receive so as to be better prepared for such emergencies.

Their traditional ways of working are co-operative, the whole community working together on each other's pieces of land; so here, with advice from CIPE, and tools loaned by them, a joint effort is under way to make a substantial trench so as to conserve the rainwater when it comes. From the deep trenches the water can seep under the surface and run down the slope to water the seeds – an easier form of irrigation than carrying water up from the river, and a more reliable method than a large number of small irrigation channels. In such ways the *campesinos* can become more self-supporting without abandoning their traditional working methods.

God of community,
when I am in a hard, dry place,
and I cannot survive alone,
help me give and receive support
from those who share my hardship.
Teach us to prepare for blessing
so that when it comes
it may soak into every part of our life,
fully used.

Psalm 104:1-13 From your lofty abode you water the mountains; the earth is satisfied with the fruit of your work. (v13)

October

Basic rights

Christian Aid/Achinto

After years of bonded labour, Sonabhai in India holds her formal certificate of release

Azazmi, Israel

'Unrecognised' communities

Pylons bring electricity – but not to the village of Azazmi, where cables carry the supply, unconnected, over the roofs of the people's houses.

You will not find Azazmi on a map: officially it doesn't exist. It is one of many Palestinian Arab villages located within the territory of Israel, but not 'recognised' by the Israeli government. Without recognition, the villagers cannot claim basic rights like piped clean water, education and health care.

The villages are 'unrecognised' because the government wants their inhabitants to leave. A chemical waste dump has been built very near Azazmi and villagers suffer from a pollution-based disease caused by the toxic chemicals. Their flocks have also been confiscated – despite the fact that generations of these people have lived on this land for hundreds of years.

A Palestinian Arab organisation called the Association of Forty works hard to get villages like Azazmi recognised, but it is a slow legal battle that takes many years. In the meantime the Association also seeks to improve life in the village communities by, for example, helping education projects, installing sewage, water and electricity systems, and improving roads.

'They have drawn up all sorts of criteria about what is and is not a village. As far as we are concerned, we are there, we exist.'

Mohammed, a resident of En Houd, one of the unrecognised villages

Christian Aid/DK Crevance

God give strength
to those who are passed over
for the necessities of life.
For you have always chosen
those who are called nothing,
of no account,
officially not there –
and with them
fashioned your will for our world.

1 Corinthians 1:25-29 God chose what is low and despised in the world, things that are not, to reduce to nothing things that are. (v28)

Christian Aid/Steve Lewis

'If we stick together we will succeed.'

Sung by the women of Boane, members of ORAM, as they greeted visitors

Mozambique

Land rights

Rural Association for Mutual Support

Like her mothers before her,
she gives this field her love, her labour;
its ditches are familiar to her feet,
she handles the seedlings gently,
estimating a harvest.
God give the produce of this fertile earth
to those who nurture and need it.

Walking alone through her rice fields, this member of Mucela, a women's co-operative farming association, knows the power of working with others. She used to walk to the market 12 miles away, having to sell her rice at whatever price she could get. With the support of ORAM, she and the other women in her association built a warehouse to store the rice so that together they now hire a tractor and trailer to take the rice to the market when prices are high.

A major problem for Mozambican peasants remains their lack of security over land. The civil war in Mozambique lasted 16 years and led to five million people being displaced. When the Peace Agreement was signed in 1992, refugees returning home found their land taken over by local entrepreneurs and by multi-nationals. They didn't know they needed a title to claim the land that has fed their families for generations.

Individual farmers cannot afford to pay for a title themselves, so they form rural associations, supported by ORAM, who lobby the government on land reform. ORAM provides legal advice and agricultural and business training to the associations, aiming to make farmers self-reliant.

Isaiah 65:21-25
They shall not plant and another eat. (v22)

India

The right to freedom

It may seem strange that young men should be playing a children's game. But the boys who come to Mukti Ashram ('Freedom House') each have terrible tales to tell of their lives as child bonded labourers in the carpet industry.

Nageshwar was five when he began his nine years of working 12-14 hours a day at a carpet loom. When he was caught helping other boys to escape he was locked in a room for three weeks. Tied, gagged and tortured, he was unable to speak when he came out – and still silent when he arrived at Mukti Ashram.

Boys fortunate enough to escape or be rescued and taken to the Ashram spend three to six months there, learning not only practical skills, like weaving and carpentry, but also how to take responsibility for their lives. Importantly, they also learn how to play – childhood comes late to those forced into the carpet factories. The organisation behind Mukti Ashram – South Asian Coalition on Child Servitude – has also initiated the 'Rugmark', a way of giving information about child-free carpet production.

Nageshwar didn't remain silent. After some time in the company of the other boys, one day he sang in a whisper a song his mother once taught him, his first words since his release: 'Never weep for a single moment in life. Always live with a smile in your heart.'

Christian Aid/Achinto

'All their lives they have been told what to do by their parents or by their masters. We try to teach them to feel responsible.'

Suman, Director of Mukti Ashram

O God, you bring light
to those who have been shut in darkness;
you bring freedom
to those who have known only bondage.
Give these young men back
the childhood they lost,
the words they were afraid to speak,
the dreams they could not afford:
let them play, and plan, and sing.

Isaiah 42:1-9
Bring out the prisoners from the dungeon, from the prison those who sit in darkness. (v7)

God of the just weight
and the fair measure,
let me remember the hands
that harvested my food, my drink,
not only in my prayers
but in the marketplace.
Let me not seek a bargain
that leaves another hungry.

Christian Aid/Harriet Logan/Network

'If it wasn't for Prodeco-op, we wouldn't have been able to afford food at all this year. The peas and beans we grow to eat were ruined by slugs so now we have to buy food. The good price we got for our coffee meant that we could afford to buy food for ourselves and our children, rather than go hungry.'

Juanita Martínez Reyes, coffee grower

Northern Nicaragua

Fair trade

Once these coffee beans are sorted, how much will they be worth?

Coffee is Nicaragua's most important export, but very little of the money paid in the UK and Ireland for a jar of coffee gets back to the small farmers who grow it. Middlemen eat up much of the profit, and world prices can change, leaving producers struggling to buy food for their families.

Growers coming together to form co-operatives have broken this unfair cycle. Prodeco-op is a marketing organisation owned by 62 coffee producers' co-operatives in northern Nicaragua. It sells the produce of local coffee growers, guaranteeing them a fair price, even offering a minimum seasonal price to overcome fluctuations in the world market. One of its customers is Cafédirect, which is sold in many supermarkets.

Because Prodeco-op also helps growers to organise their own transportation and processing, instead of a profit of a few pence per pound of coffee, they now make some 20 pence per pound. As a result, they are able to support their families and become free of debt. Prodeco-op also advises them on things like pest control and organic growing, which offers an even better harvest and income.

Deuteronomy 24:15 You shall pay them their wages daily before sunset, because they are poor and their livelihood depends on them.

November

Land and environment

Christian Aid/Tom Learmonth

Pas Baria, a coastal area of Bangladesh prone to flooding and cyclones

Antonia Ebuenga skilfully guides his small and unstable dugout canoe among the mangroves as he looks for where to leave the crab pots today.

Antonia has been helped by the work of Tambuyog, a name which comes from 'tambuye', a conch shell traditionally used to call fishermen in from the sea. Tambuyog, a non-governmental organisation, aims to create self-sufficient communities who can control and manage the natural coastal resources that offer them a livelihood but without using methods that destroy habitats.

In this case, it has meant overcoming the destruction of the mangrove swamps when the trees were cut down for fish farming. It happened when the government offered cheap 25-year leases on fish farms, with the aim of exporting fish and prawns to acquire foreign currency.

But now the trees have been replanted (it takes 30,000 seedlings for each hectare) and the crabs are back. Antonia sells the small 'seed' crabs he catches on to other pond owners. The mature crabs go direct to market. They don't earn Antonia very much, but the return of the mangroves makes it possible for him, his four children, their own children, and the local coastal community, to survive.

Christian Aid/Alberto Garcia

God of all creation,
in your teeming and orderly world,
we have disturbed the balance –
the rich forcing the poor
to wreck environments.
Help us renew the landscape,
restoring what has been destroyed,
so that life may continue,
precarious, but able to endure.

'In the mid 1980s
the mangroves were
completely cut down...
a disaster for us because
the crabs live off the
special microenvironment
created by the mangrove
root. In the last seven years
much of the mangrove
has been replanted
by us. With the mangroves
the crabs have returned.'

Vincente Desolo

Prieto Diaz,

Philippines

Restored habitats

Psalm 104:14-35 The earth is full of your creatures.
Yonder is the sea, great and wide, creeping things innumerable are there. (v24-25)

Christian Aid/Salomon Cytrynowicz

Brazil

Claiming unproductive land

'To build freedom has a price. No one can be settled without a fight, even death, yes, some die in the struggle and many more die of hunger.'

Raminho, Movement for the Landless

O Lord,
you had nowhere to lay your head.
Remember all those on this earth
who sleep by the roadside,
who have no place to stay,
no patch of ground to call their own.
Give them a secure space,
where no one may remove them:
a place to work and raise children,
hang out the washing,
and be at home.

There's something about a washing line anywhere in the world that speaks of 'home'. This one belongs to Clemente José and his family who live on Fazenda Paixão (Farm of the Passion).

The name of their farm derives from the date on which they first occupied the land. It was in 1992, when a group of families came by night on the Thursday before Easter and took over a patch of dusty scrubland near an airport. Like thousands of other landless people in Brazil they made shelters out of sheets of black plastic, started to settle and claimed legal rights to the disused land.

Brazil is a wealthy country, but its riches are for the few. Three-quarters of the people in rural Brazil have no land and most of those families cannot adequately feed their children.

Under the Brazilian constitution, it is legal to occupy and settle on land that is idle (up to 42 per cent of rural land in Brazil). Movimento Sem Terra – the Movement for the Landless – was founded in 1985 and seeks to help groups of landless people claim legal rights to such land. This is seldom achieved without violent struggle against powerful landowners. But when such groups get official title of the land, Sem Terra helps them develop good farming practice and the co-operative methods they will need to survive.

Amos 9:15 I will plant them upon their land, and they shall never again be plucked up out of the land I have given them.

In the evening light, this farmer standing on his field looks prosperous enough. But this is Gaza, the narrow coastal strip where nearly one million Palestinians live, mostly crowded into long-term refugee camps. Some Palestinians who owned land here have lost it to Israeli settlements, or to the security zone surrounding a settlement.

Ashour El Laham has land, but his face is lined with anxiety. Access to export markets is virtually impossible in this cut-off zone. Even the fresh water supply for his crops is scarce and salty, since the Israelis' deep artesian wells have overused the underground water supply, causing sea water to pollute it. In these hard conditions Ashour and other farmers appreciate the work of the Palestinian Agricultural Relief Committees (PARC), which aim to help rural communities become sustainable economic units.

Water issues and food security are PARC's priorities. Desalinating techniques are taught, and rainwater saved in every possible way: a solar pump is used to carry water, collected in concrete 'ponds' from greenhouse run-offs, into overground pipes such as these on Ashour's field. Many serious problems remain, but some farmers are at least learning ways of becoming self-sufficient in a very difficult situation.

The earth is yours, O Lord,
and all its abundance.
You send the rain to water it,
making it produce life
and sprout new shoots of hope.
May the ground bear good fruit,
and the people bring forth justice.
Send us rain, O Lord,
but also send us righteousness.

Gaza Strip,
Palestinian Territories

The politics of water

'We are trying to
harvest the rainfall.'

Palestinian farmer

Christian Aid/DK Crevance

Hosea 10:12 Break up your fallow ground; for it is time to seek the Lord, that he may come and rain righteousness upon you.

Christian Aid/Sara Burns

O God, you have promised
that the meek shall inherit the earth.
May the voice of the poorest,
who need the forest to live in,
be heard above the clamour
of those who just want to make money,
so that all our grandchildren
may have the earth's beauty to share.

Pacific Coast region, Colombia

Threat to the rainforest

Happy children, proud grandmother, beautiful land: but Lorgia Condé lives in the poorest region of a developing country where the extraction of natural resources is the easiest and swiftest route to financial gain.

The Pacific coastal area of Colombia, cut off from the rest of the country by a high spur of the Andes, is a land of dense forests and many rivers, and the population of indigenous peoples and Afro-Colombians have for centuries been largely left alone to their subsistence farming. But this area, so rich in mineral resources and other opportunities for quick development by international companies, has become the 'money box' of the Colombian state, the subject of national planning that shows many signs of ignoring the rights of its inhabitants. Already large swathes of the rainforest have been felled, and extensive roadbuilding, hydro-electric and other projects have led to sustained counter-planning, as the local peoples have joined forces to present their case for development that respects their rights to land, and their culture.

Christian Aid supports the work of the Regional Indigenous Organisation of the Chocó of the Emberá-Wounaan (OREWA) and the Indigenous Organisation of Antioquia (OIA) in their joint programme for alternative development.

'We believe we are part of nature, not separate from it. The Indian is totally embroiled in the tropical rainforest, its trees, its animals, its birds, rivers, fish, rain, sun, air, flowers... Everything that happens to the earth will happen to the children of the earth. And that doesn't just mean the indigenous peoples, it means you here.'

Euclides Peña, indigenous leader

Luke 12:15 Be on your guard against all kinds of greed; for one's life does not consist in the abundance of possessions.

December

Health

Christian Aid/Elaine Duigenan

A 50-bed hospital at
Milo in Tanzania

Christian Aid/Betty East

When I come to die,
give me companions:
cheerful, practical,
able to walk the edge with me
and look me in the eye.
Until that time,
grant me to use fully
each day, each hour,
open-hearted, knowing your love,
savouring my life.

Ndola diocese, Zambia

Caring at home

Dorothy, a health worker, is holding the basic equipment you need when you look after someone with HIV and AIDS-related illnesses at home.

AIDS is devastating the countries of southern Africa. In Zambia, it is estimated that one in four sexually active adults is HIV positive. AIDS affects all of life, and young adults, who tend to be the main wage-earners, are the most vulnerable to HIV infection.

Mary was only 24 when she died of AIDS. Her husband, through whom she probably became infected, had left home. Both of her children had died. Mary lived with her brother and sister, the three of them earning a living selling sweet potatoes and charcoal. During her last difficult months of life, Mary and her family were visited regularly by Edith Banda, a volunteer from Ndola Catholic Diocese AIDS programme.

The work of the AIDS programme is vital in a country where the few hospitals are already overcrowded and many people cannot afford the cost of medical care. With the support of health workers like Dorothy and trained volunteers like Edith, families are helped to look after their own relatives within their own communities.

'I have eight children of my own, I am a grandmother. Throughout my community, sick adults are coming home to die. I could have got a job with an income – we need the money – but I wanted to do this work instead.'

Edith Banda

Matthew 25:31-45
I was sick and you took care of me. (v36)

Mare Rouge, Haiti

Infant nutrition

'The help we need is not eternal. It is a source of humiliation to people who know how to work, that however hard they work they do not get anywhere. For the future of our children we need help at the moment... our work is to say, "Yes there is hope. While people are alive there is hope."'

Fr Burnet Chérisol, Director of Child Care Haiti

To look out beyond the doorway is to look out at a land ravaged by severe drought and a loss of trees that has led to poor soil and increasingly desert-like conditions.
Last year the harvest in this remote region of north-west Haiti failed for the third time running. There was a sharp rise in infant malnutrition and women were having to walk up to three hours to collect water, in some cases only to spend a day queuing to fill their buckets.

Mare Rouge is located in the heart of the north west, an area commonly known as the 'far-west' and considered to be one of the most destitute areas in Haiti.

The organisation Child Care Haiti runs a number of nutritional centres which focus in particular on children aged 0-5 years. As well as distributing food, and milk enriched with oil and sugar, the Centre also provides a programme training women to monitor children's health and nutrition, sessions on preventative health care, and some basic medical and dental equipment.

Christian Aid/Leah Gordon

God of the desert places
be with those who wait,
queuing for water and food
watching their little children
lose energy to play,
looking for rain,
for work and health and harvest.
In their time of waiting,
be their hearts' courage
and their souls' hope;
make their desert bloom.

Psalm 130:1-6 I wait for the Lord, my soul waits,
and in his word I hope; my soul waits for the Lord. (v5-6)

Tamil Nadu, South India

Traditional medicine

Christian Aid/Jamie Drummond

'If wealth is lost,
nothing is lost.
If health is lost,
everything is lost.'

Local proverb

Not what we usually think of as a medicine cabinet, but the herbal garden in Kelaveliyur where Punamal is working will supply, with the right knowledge to use them, all sorts of plants and herbs for traditional remedies. It is a powerful image of taking responsibility for one's own health.

SEVAI – the Society for Education, Village Action and Improvement – encourages villagers in the Trichy district of Tamil Nadu to improve their own health and nutrition. It runs both a mobile rural health programme and a health centre to provide more accessible health care.

But at the same time, wanting to stress the importance of preventative care and the value of traditional ways, it holds training camps to promote the use of herbal medicine and encourages women to grow their own kitchen gardens.

To promote good nutrition, especially in pregnant and nursing mothers and in small children, SEVAI has introduced 'live fencing'. This means that gardens are fenced with good hybrid fruit trees – varieties like mango, coconut, pomegranate, lemon, cherry and guava. Other plants can be used for traditional remedies, for instance toloso, which is good for colds, and amarpardiasi, which encourages mothers to produce more milk for their babies. The small sign in the foreground suggests caution, however: it reads 'Poison'!

God of beauty,
maker of all that grows,
you did not create us
to be separate from this earth,
but planted us in a garden
to tend it and care for it.
We thank you for the multitude of plants
that nourish our bodies,
comfort our pain
and give us pleasure.

Ezekiel 47:12
Their fruit will be for food and their leaves for healing.

South-west Tanzania

Giving birth

'The debt burden is killing people because people cannot afford to go to the hospital. If they don't have drugs, they die. It is a direct result of the debt crisis.'

Canon HP Mtingele, General Secretary of the Church of the Province of Tanzania

New life, new hope. But what sort of life and what sort of hope?

Children born in countries like Tanzania, that are staggering under the weight of their foreign debt, are not exactly born into slavery. But neither are they born free, because the impact of that debt will affect their lives for the worse from their very first breath. Technically, this baby already owes £120 to foreign governments.

Just delivered by Caesarean section in Milo Hospital in south-west Tanzania, he is Prisca Mhagama's first baby. Prisca lives with her parents in Ludende village, some six miles from Milo. Only 17, she walked to the hospital with her mother and will walk back again in nine days' time when she has had her stitches taken out.

Prisca's stay in hospital has not been free. Governments deeply in debt can not afford properly to subsidise health care. So Prisca's father will be faced with a bill that will probably force him to sell some of his precious goats.

Although Prisca was nervous and tearful when she arrived at the hospital, she is confident about looking after the baby because of what she has learned at the ante-natal clinic, part of the community-based health education programme that Christian Aid funds through the Church of the Province of Tanzania.

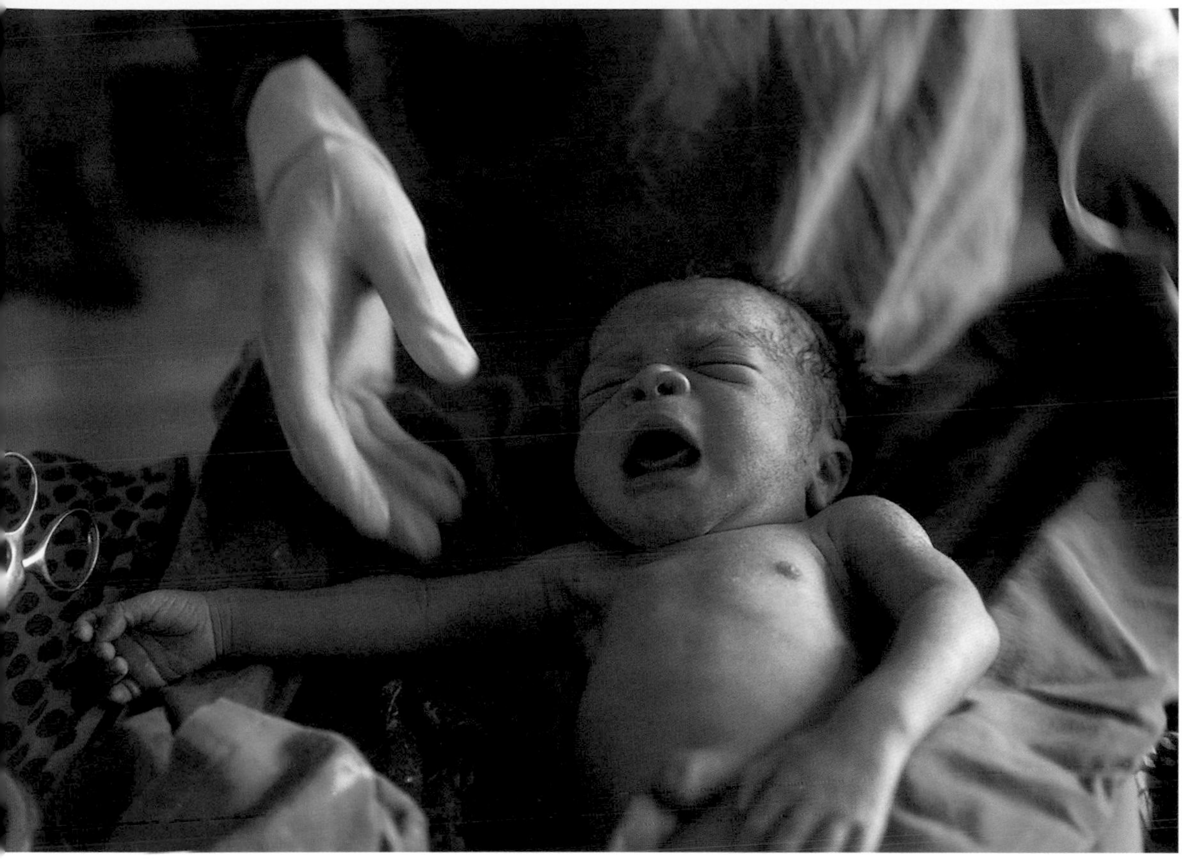

Christian Aid/Elaine Duigenan

Christ our God,
you too were born a child
not free into our world:
subject to poverty,
harassment by foreign powers,
and dangers to your health.
In your name
let us cry freedom for your children
now, at this time,
and through all generations.

Isaiah 65:17-23
They shall not labour in vain, or bear children for calamity. (v23)

Haiti
Dominican Republic
Mali
Honduras
The Gambia
Nicaragua
Sierra Leone
Ghana
Colombia
Peru
Bolivia
Brazil

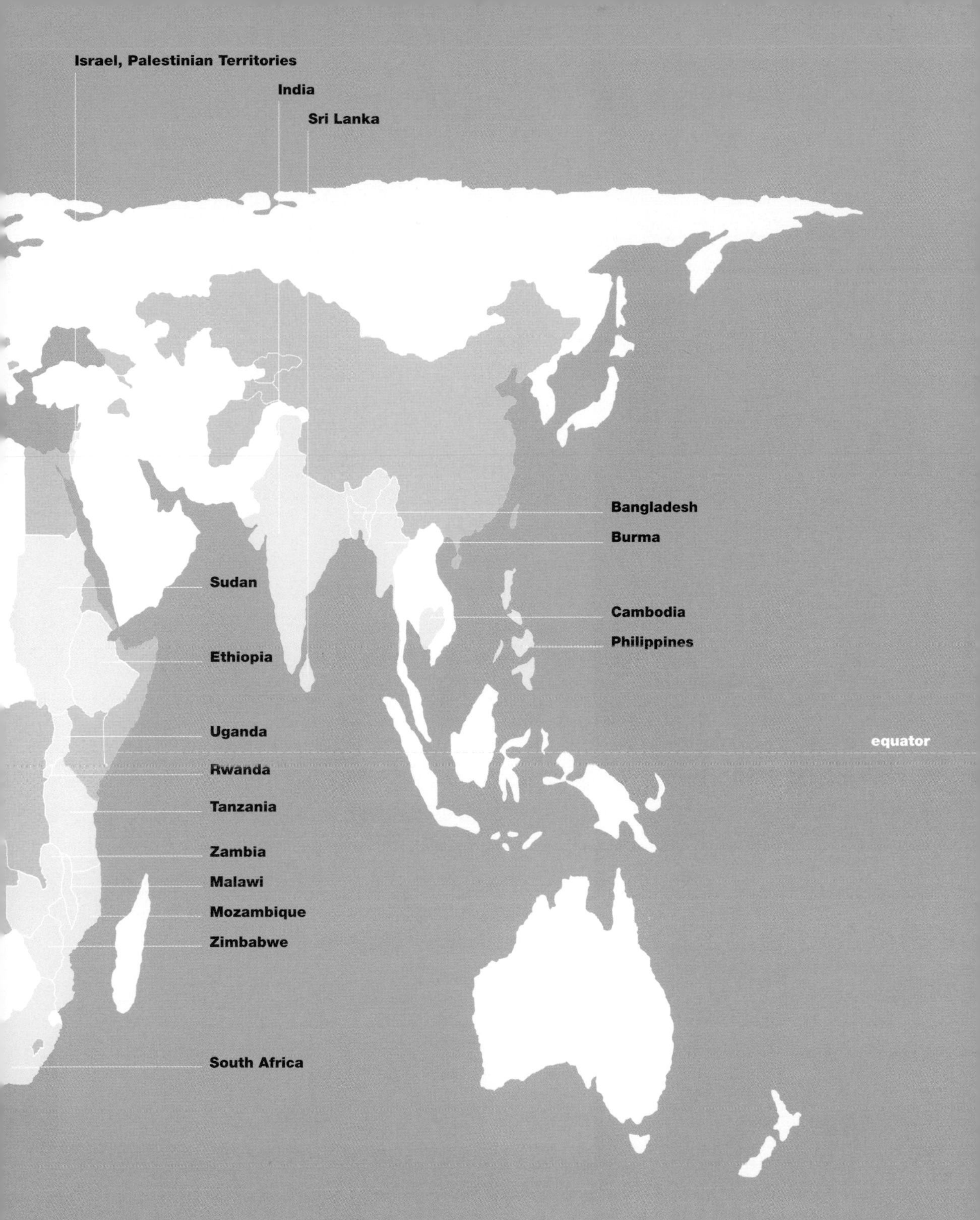

Countries featured in this book

Countries where Christian Aid also supports work

Other ways to respond

Christian Aid values your prayers for its work. But if you are ready and able to get involved in other ways, please get in touch. For details about any of the following, ring Supporter Relations on 0171 523 2315.

Learning more

Christian Aid News is a colourful magazine, produced three times a year, which is full of readable up-to-date stories about communities across the world whom Christian Aid supports. It is sent free of charge and includes further prayer suggestions.

Campaigning for change

Christian Aid runs major campaigns which seek to engage people's influence as consumers or citizens to press for changes in commercial practices or government policies which will benefit the world's poor. You can receive regular information about the current campaign, which will explain how you and your church can get involved and really make a difference.

Giving money

We can only do the work if people continue to be generous. There are many ways, both through one-off gifts and through regular donations, that you can help guarantee the income we need so that we can support more poor communities. There are ways to give, especially around the turn of the millennium, which enable us to reclaim tax from the government.

Getting involved locally

Christian Aid is an organisation that depends on its strong and capable volunteer base. You can help in many ways: by collecting in Christian Aid Week, the annual house-to-house fundraising effort in May; by helping organise local events to raise funds or to encourage greater awareness of global issues; or by offering your particular skills as a contract volunteer if you can commit time on a regular basis. Contact your local Christian Aid organiser, or if you don't know who this is, ring Supporter Relations to find out.